BENJAMIN WHITE

LITERARY ANALYSIS HANDBOOK

Unlocking English and Literature

Published in 2024 by Amba Press, Melbourne, Australia
www.ambapress.com.au

© Benjamin White 2024

All rights reserved. No part of this book may be reproduced or transmitted in any form or by any means, electronic or mechanical, including photocopying, recording or by any information storage and retrieval system, without prior permission in writing from the publisher.

Cover design: Tess McCabe
Editor: Rica Dearman
Some of the images have been generated using AI.

ISBN: 9781923116597 (pbk)
ISBN: 9781923116603 (ebk)

A catalogue record for this book is available from the National Library of Australia.

Contents

Introduction to literary analysis		1
Chapter 1	Elements of literature	9
Chapter 2	Figurative language and literary devices	19
Chapter 3	Literary movements and genres	27
Chapter 4	Unpacking form and meaning	35
Chapter 5	Literature in context	43
Chapter 6	Critical approaches to literature	51
Chapter 7	Adapting and transforming literature	59
Chapter 8	Writing a literary analysis	65
Chapter 9	Responding creatively to literature	69
Chapter 10	Preparing for your exam	73
Conclusion		77

Introduction to literary analysis

Let's be honest, the reason you're here is because your English or Literature teacher has spent weeks on end banging on about some text you're studying and now you must present *something* on it – maybe an essay, maybe a visual essay, maybe a creative response. Whichever form you end up choosing – and we'll cover these later – the core of your task will be on ***analysis***. But what exactly do we, and I mean 'we' because I am one of those English and Literature teachers, mean by literary analysis?

Understanding literary analysis

Literary analysis is an essential skill for any student of English and Literature. It is the process of examining, dissecting and understanding a piece of literature to gain a deeper appreciation and comprehension of its components, themes and messages, as well as its views, values and ideas. It's not just about *what* the text says, but *how* it says it and *why* it matters.

At its core, literary analysis is a conversation between the reader and the text. It's a dialogue that seeks to uncover the layers of meaning that an author has woven into their work. As high school students, you are not just passive receivers of this information; you are active participants in the exploration and interpretation of literature.

The purpose of literary analysis

Why do we analyse literature? What's the point in all of this? The simple answer is that we analyse literature to understand it better. But it's something more than that – all works of literature are products of their time. They reflect the ideas, views and values of the period or era. Moreover, literature reflects our shared humanity: our thoughts, our fears, our dreams and our histories. By analysing literature, we gain insights into the human condition, into different cultures, into historical contexts and into diverse perspectives.

On top of all that, literary analysis develops critical thinking skills. It encourages you to question, to probe and to consider multiple viewpoints. In a world swamped with information, and fake news and deepfakes, these skills are especially important. These skills will allow you to evaluate sources carefully and form well-reasoned opinions.

> **Key tip:** Avoid simply summarising the plot! Analysis requires examining *how* and *why* elements of literature operate, not just stating what happens.

Approaches to literary analysis

There is no single *right* way of analysing a piece of literature, but there are several critical lenses you can use to guide your analysis. We'll dig into these, and other lenses, a little deeper in Chapter 6. But first, here are the different approaches you can use to analyse literature:

1. **Formalist approach:** This method focuses on the form of the literature – its structure, language and literary devices. It asks *how* the author uses these elements to create meaning.

2. **Historical approach:** This approach considers the historical context of the work. What was happening in the world when the text was written? How did these events influence the author and their writing?

3. **Psychoanalytical approach:** This approach delves into the psychological aspects of the literature, often examining characters' motivations, desires and conflicts.

4. **Sociological approach:** This method examines the social context of the work, exploring themes like class, race, gender and power dynamics.

5. **Reader-response approach:** This approach focuses on your personal response to the text. It acknowledges that each reader brings their own experiences and emotions to their interpretation. The sum total of your life's experiences impacts how you view characters and events.

Elements of literary analysis

When analysing a piece of literature, several key elements come into play:

1. **Plot:** The sequence of events in a story. How are these events structured? Is the plot linear or non-linear?

2. **Characters:** The individuals in the story. What are their motivations, strengths, weaknesses? How do they evolve over the course of the narrative?

3. **Setting:** The time and place where the story occurs. How does the setting influence the characters and the plot?

4. **Point of view:** The perspective from which the story is told. Is it first person, second person or third person? How does this viewpoint shape the story?

5. **Theme:** The central idea or message of the story. What is the author trying to communicate? How is this theme conveyed?

Literary devices

Authors use various literary devices to enhance their storytelling and add deeper meaning. Some of these include:

- **Metaphor and simile:** Comparisons used to add depth and understanding to characters, settings or situations.
- **Symbolism:** The use of symbols to represent ideas or qualities.
- **Irony:** A contrast between expectation and reality, often highlighting the complexity of truth.
- **Foreshadowing:** Hints or clues about what will happen later in the story.
- **Imagery:** Descriptive language that appeals to the senses, creating vivid mental pictures.

> **Key tip:** Use textual evidence from the work itself to support your analytical claims.

Basic structure

This is the basic structure of a literary analysis essay. No doubt you've come across this before in your study of English or Literature, but here it is again:

1. **Introduction:** Information about the text and author and your main contention (the point you're arguing).
2. **Body paragraphs (the classic example is three):**
   a. *What* your paragraph is about, and how it ties back to your main contention.
   b. *How* the text supports your argument. You'll put textual evidence here (quotes, examples of literary devices, plot events).
   c. *Why* the evidence supports your main contention. Why you chose it to support your points. This is your analysis and interpretation. It's your time to shine.
   d. *So*, why is this important? How your paragraph ties back to your main contention and the point you're trying to make.
3. **Conclusion:** Restate your main contention (using different words, to keep it interesting for your reader/assessor), summarise your key points and add your final thoughts on the text.

Practising literary analysis

To develop your skills in literary analysis, practice is key. Start by reading (yes, reading the text) actively and critically. Ask questions as you read: Why did the author choose this word? What is the significance of this event? How do the character's actions impact the overall story?

Take notes and annotate the text. Highlight passages that stand out, jot down thoughts and questions in the margins. Discussion with others can also be incredibly valuable. Literature is a shared experience, and different perspectives offer new insights.

Finally, remember that there is no single right answer in literary analysis. You can essentially say what you like about the text, so long as you back it up with the text. Literary analysis is about building a well-supported interpretation based on the text. Your perspective is unique, and your analysis will reflect that.

This is what you probably don't like about English – there's no right answer. The 'right' answer lies in your ability to argue your point, using the text. What you see in the text will be different from what I see in the text, versus what your teacher sees in the text. This, at its core, is the great thing about studying literature – every person who reads it breathes new life into it.

Activity: Snack-sized literary analysis

Now that you have an introduction to literary analysis, choose a short story to practise these new skills. Some short story recommendations:

- *The Story of an Hour* by Kate Chopin
- *The Most Dangerous Game* by Richard Connell
- *The Necklace* by Guy de Maupassant
- *Harrison Bergeron* by Kurt Vonnegut

Step 1: Annotate

Make notes and annotate as you read. Mark passages that stand out, and jot down your thoughts in the margins.

Step 2: Ask questions

Analyse the text by asking questions:

1. What is the plot structure? Is there evidence of foreshadowing?
2. How would you describe the main character? Do they undergo any changes?
3. What is the setting? Does the period or location play an important role?
4. What are some prominent themes in the text? What message might the author be exploring?

Step 3: Literary devices

Identify some literary devices the author employs. Consider metaphors, imagery, irony or symbolism. How do these stylistic choices contribute to a deeper meaning?

Step 4: Mini analysis

Choose one element you found intriguing to focus on for a mini literary analysis. This could be the imagery around a certain motif, a character's transformation, the use of irony, the story's themes.

Step 5: Write

Write a paragraph on your chosen element using the structure listed in this introduction.

CHAPTER 1

Elements of literature

Literature is an art form that uses words to create worlds, tell stories, express emotions and convey ideas. To understand and appreciate literature, it's crucial to grasp its basic elements: plot, character, setting, point of view and theme. These elements are the building blocks of any literary work, from epic novels to short poems. In this chapter, we'll explore each of these elements in detail.

Plot

The plot is the sequence of events that make up the story. It's what happens from the beginning of the story to the end. Typically, plots have a structure that includes an introduction (or exposition), rising action, climax, falling action and resolution (or, to be super fancy, *denouement*). You may have seen this represented as a pyramid, or in your primary school days, as the 'story mountain'.

The Story Mountain

1. **Introduction:** This is where the story begins, setting the scene and introducing the characters and the initial situation.
2. **Rising action:** Here, the story builds up. Conflicts and challenges faced by the characters are developed.
3. **Climax:** The turning point of the story, often the most exciting part, where the main conflict reaches its peak.
4. **Falling action:** The aftermath of the climax, where conflict starts moving towards resolution.
5. **Resolution:** The end of the story, where conflicts are resolved and the story concludes.

Different plot structures

Not all plots conform to the traditional linear, chronological order. Complex narrative structures in modern literature play with the presentation of events through techniques like flashbacks, flashforwards and other non-linear approaches. No doubt the text you're currently studying has a non-linear plot because English and Literature teachers loves a non-linear plot.

Linear plot structure
- The most straightforward plot structure, where events happen in chronological order. This structure is easy to follow and allows for a clear progression of the story.

Non-linear structure
- Involves a disruption of the chronological flow of the story. It might include flashbacks, flashforwards or a fragmented sequence of events. This structure can create suspense or provide a deeper understanding of characters and events.

Circular plot structure
- The story ends where it began. This structure often emphasises the themes of fate, destiny or the unchanging nature of certain aspects of life.

In medias res
- Latin for 'in the middle of things', this structure starts the story in the middle of the action, often skipping the traditional introduction. The earlier parts of the story are later filled in through flashbacks or dialogue.

Frame narrative
- A story within a story, where the main narrative is presented as part of a story told by a narrator within the story. This can add layers of complexity and perspective to the narrative.

Parallel plot structure

- Involves multiple storylines, often involving different characters, that run parallel to each other and may intersect at various points. This structure allows for a multifaceted look at themes and events.

Episodic plot structure

- The story is divided into a series of episodes or segments, each somewhat self-contained, but contributing to the overall narrative. This structure is common in serialised novels and television series.

Character

Characters are the individuals in a story. They can be people, animals or even imaginary creatures. Characters are crucial because they drive the plot and engage the reader's emotions and interest. There are several types of characters:

Protagonist

Antagonist

Minor characters

- **Protagonist:** The main character around whom the story revolves.
- **Antagonist:** The character or force that opposes the protagonist.
- **Minor characters:** Characters who play secondary roles in the story, helping to advance the plot or develop the protagonist.

Character analysis involves investigating traits, motivations, background stories, transformations over time and the significance tied to a figure's words, thoughts and actions.

Setting

The setting represents where and when the events of literature take place. This backdrop contextualises narratives for readers through exact time periods and geographic locations. Settings also provide cultural, political, economic and social context. Characters explicitly interact with elements of a story's environment. Moreover, elements of setting equally underscore a tale's atmosphere through weather, landscapes, technology, architecture, cityscapes, etc.

Consider J.K. Rowling's Harry Potter series. Hogwarts is an old, mysterious, dimly lit castle, which adds to the journey of self-discovery that Harry and his wizard pals go on. The feel of Harry Potter would be different if it was set in a cold, fluorescent-lit high school in the middle of London. Like, where's the intrigue? Where's the fun?

Point of view

The point of view (POV) is the perspective from which a story is told. It determines what the reader knows about the events of the story. The main types of point of view are:

1. **First person:** The narrator is the character in the story, using 'I' or 'we'.

2. **Second person:** The narrator addresses the reader as 'you'. This is less common in literature. It's more reserved for instructional texts. But that doesn't mean you won't come across it.

3. **Third person:** The narrator is outside the story, using 'he', 'she' or 'they'. This can be omniscience (all-knowing) or limited to the perspective of one character. This is sometimes referred to as a 'God narrator' because they have access to all the thoughts, feelings, actions and information of the characters.

The type of narrator impacts how reality in the text is perceived. Unreliable narrators display limited, biased story information to readers. Meanwhile, omniscient narrators possess complete knowledge of all plot points and characters' interior lives. What's the narrator like in your text? Is it unreliable? How do you know?

Theme

English and Literature teachers love to talk about the *theme* of the text. It's what the story is about, beyond its plot and characters. Themes can explore universal concepts like love, war, friendship, betrayal and morality. A text can have one or multiple themes. Identifying the theme involves looking at the events, characters and setting in the story and what larger ideas they may represent.

Views and values

Literature is also a reflection of the views and values of its time and of the author. By presenting certain perspectives, authors can challenge readers to question their own beliefs and the norms of society.

- **Views:** These are the opinions or perspectives expressed in a literary work. They can be the author's own perspectives or those of the characters. For example, a novel set in a dystopian future may reflect views on government control or individual freedom.

- **Values:** These are the moral principles that are evident in a story. Values can be explicit, like the importance of honesty in a moral fable, or implicit, such as the value of courage in a hero's journey.

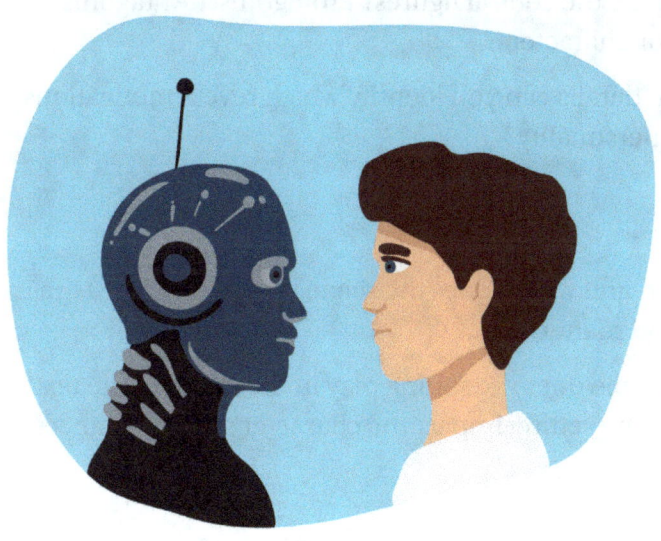

Activity: Applying your analytical lenses

Using the text you're studying, or one of the story recommendations listed in the introduction, practise identifying the fundamental elements. Select a short passage filled with sensory details, something you can really get into.

Plot:

- What sequence of events do you notice? Do flashbacks/forwards appear?
- Where does the passage fall on the plot pyramid: exposition, rising action, climax?

Characters:

- Who are the central figures? Protagonist? Antagonist? Minor characters?
- What details can you identify which reveal motivations and personality?

Setting:

- When and where does the scene take place? Does the period matter?
- What role does the setting play in the mood of the text? Does the setting impact the character's circumstances?

POV:

- Whose perspective guides your reading?
- Is the narrator reliable? Do they have limited or omniscient access to the events?

Themes:

♦ What themes arise in the passage? How do they relate to the human experience/condition?

Now choose two of these elements to analyse more deeply:

♦ Find textual evidence to support your claims and explain *how* it supports your claims.

♦ Discuss what deeper significance these elements contribute to the wider text.

CHAPTER 2

Figurative language and literary devices

In this chapter we will explore how and why authors use figurative language and literary devices to enrich their writing to immerse readers in their texts.

What is figurative language?

Figurative language is a way of using words and phrases that deviates from their literal interpretation to convey a more complex, insightful or vivid idea. Unlike literal language, which states facts directly, figurative language invites the reader to imagine and infer. It is the author's ways of *showing* the story, not *telling* the story.

1. **Similes and metaphors**

    Two of the most common figurative language tools are similes and metaphors. No doubt you've come across these in your early high school years (that Year 7 poetry unit perhaps, which I'm sure you loved). Both similes and metaphors do the same thing, essentially: they both compare one thing to another.

    - **Simile:** A simile uses 'like' or 'as' to compare two different things, highlighting similarities between them. For example, 'Her smile was as bright as the sun'. This simile compares a smile to the sun, suggesting it is very bright and cheerful.

- **Metaphor:** A metaphor, on the other hand, states that one thing is another, helping to create a vivid mental picture. For example, 'Time is a thief'. Here, time is not literally a thief running around taking numbers off clocks. Instead, this metaphor suggests that it steals moments from us.

2. **Personification:** Personification gives human qualities to non-human things. For example, 'The wind whispered through the trees'. The wind can't whisper, but this gives a sensory feeling to its movement.

3. **Hyperbole:** Hyperbole is an intentional exaggeration for emphasis or humour. 'I'm so hungry I could eat a horse' is an extreme exaggeration used to convey strong hunger.

4. **Alliteration:** Alliteration is the repetition of initial consonant sounds across several words in a phrase or sentence. For example, 'Peter Piper picked a peck of pickled peppers'. The repetition of the 'p' sound creates an auditory effect that can make the phrase more memorable and attention-grabbing.

5. **Onomatopoeia:** Onomatopoeia refers to words whose sound is very close to or imitates the sound they refer to. Words like 'boom', 'buzz' and 'crackle' are examples, as they evoke the feeling of the actual sound. For example, 'The fire crackled and popped loudly in the fireplace'.

6. **Oxymoron:** An oxymoron combines two normally contradictory terms to suggest an unexpectedly apt new meaning. For example, the phrase 'deafening silence' combines the notions of sound and quiet together for a paradoxical effect.

What are literary devices?

Literary devices are techniques that writers use to express their ideas, enhance their writing and guide readers' thoughts. Some common literary devices are:

1. **Imagery:** Imagery involves using descriptive language to create a picture in the reader's mind. It appeals to the senses. For example, 'The fresh and juicy orange is very cold and sweet'. This description appeals to the taste, touch and sight.

2. **Symbolism:** Symbolism occurs when a word, character or an object represents something beyond its literal meaning. For example, a dove often symbolises peace, a rose symbolises love.

3. **Irony:** Irony is when there is a contrast between expectation and reality. This includes verbal irony (saying the opposite of what you mean), situational irony (when the opposite of what's expected happens) and dramatic irony (when the audience knows something the characters do not).

4. **Foreshadowing:** Foreshadowing is a hint or clue about what will happen later in the story. It builds anticipation and adds layers to the narrative. For example, a character finding a mysterious key early in the story might hint at a locked door or secret later.

5. **Flashback:** This is a device where the narrative goes back in time to relay events that happened before the current point of the story. It's useful for providing background information about characters or events.

6. **Foil:** A foil is a character who contrasts with another character – usually the protagonist – to highlight qualities of the other character. For instance, a calm and collected character can serve as a foil to a hot-tempered protagonist.

7. **Under/overstatement:** Downplaying or magnifying an idea for ironic effect. For example, understating love by saying 'I don't dislike you' for comedic impact.

Purpose of figurative language and literary devices

Writers carefully and deliberately use figurative language and literary devices when constructing their texts to elevate their writing. Some of the major reasons why, include:

- **Enhance meaning:** Rather than just stating ideas literally, figurative language like metaphor and symbolism allows writers to convey more complex concepts indirectly by making surprising comparisons and substitutions. This leads to a richer reading experience and gives readers space for interpretation.

- **Create imagery:** Devices like imagery, onomatopoeia and personification place readers into palpable scenes by evoking sensory details. This makes the fictional world feel tangible and draws readers deeply into an experiential scene rather than passive narration.

- **Add depth:** Techniques like irony and oxymoron introduce contradictions that add dimensionality to texts. By subverting expectations and natural logic, writers prompt analysis and wonder that yields multilayered depth.

- **Engage readers:** Creative comparisons, surprising contradictions and heavy sensory imagery add intrigue and dynamism to texts. The unpredictability keeps readers actively engaged in the unfolding plot.

Examining writers' choices

Rather than relying on straightforward, everyday language to convey their ideas, authors deliberately choose to use figurative language, imagery, symbolism and contradictions. They don't do this to give English and Literature teachers a job, and a soapbox to get on, they do it to evoke emotional responses, impressions and intrigue in their readers. Mainly, they want you to enjoy the book, and some spicy language helps with that.

When analysing your text, consider what emotional responses your author is trying to provoke through techniques like:

- **Metaphors:** What similarities might readers need to infer between the two ideas being compared? Do the metaphors anchor to broader legends, idioms or archetypes related to the text's social context?

- **Imagery:** Imagery bombards readers with sensory details to make fictional settings seem real and visceral. As you read your text, consider how sensory descriptions immerse you in palpable, vividly rendered scenes and settings.

- **Subverted expectations:** Authors deliberately try to undermine what readers assume will logically happen in a scene or narrative. By subverting reader expectations, writers prompt responses like shock over something unexpectedly traumatic. As you read, consider how the author of your text is attempting to subvert your expectations and manipulate you into feeling something.

- **Compressed language:** Authors condense language to impart key details. Poets are good at this. They explore expansive concepts through brief, charged lines instead of long paragraphs. An example of this kind of thing might be an author using a noun like 'abyss', which hints at more danger and peril, than the basic 'hole'.

Activity: Painting with words

Choose a scene from the text you're studying. This scene should feature lots of imagery, figurative language and literary devices; something you can really get your teeth into.

Step 1: Analyse the scene's imagery

- What sensory details stand out the most? Visual details? Sounds that echo?
- Do any metaphors or similes offer surprising connections between images and ideas?
- Note any other figurative devices that contribute to an immersive, atmospheric experience.

Step 2: Create an imaginary scene

Now it's your turn to paint a compelling imaginary scene using the same techniques. You have artistic licence to create your original setting however you like, be it fantastical or every day.

Consider which environment you might create. Here are some thought-starters:

- Breezy meadow
- Packed stadium
- Secret treehouse hangout
- Underground lair

Step 3: Craft vivid imagery through figurative devices

- Incorporate at least three metaphors comparing objects to ideas.
- Use two examples of personification to bring your location to life.

- Include examples of devices like hyperbole, alliteration, etc.
- Write sections that appeal to multiple senses, using precise nouns (you may need a dictionary or thesaurus) and sensory verbs.

Step 4: Peer review

Share your scene with someone. Discuss what figurative devices proved the most transportive and why. Which part of the scene came most alive through your deliberate, authorial choices?

CHAPTER 3

Literary movements and genres

Understanding literary movements and genres is crucial for any student of literature. This chapter will explore various literary movements and genres, providing insight into how they have shaped the world of literature. Literary movements are periods marked by shared characteristics of style, subject and ideology, while genres are categories of literature defined by similar patterns, themes or formats.

Literary movements

Understanding literary movements is important for situating when and where your text was produced, and the prevailing thinking of the time. Over the page is a short list of literary movements. This is not exhaustive, the movements break up into other movements, overlap and there's some debate around when each one starts and finishes. Nevertheless, this should give you some food for thought.

Neoclassicism (mid-17th to late 18th century)

- Influenced by classical Greek and Roman art and culture.
- Neoclassicism emphasised order, logic and restrained emotion.
- Key figures include Alexander Pope and Jonathan Swift.
- This movement valued clarity, reason and harmony, often reflected in satires and heroic couplets in poetry.

Romanticism (late 18th to mid-19th century)

- Marked by an emphasis on emotion, indvidualism and a deep appreciation of nature.
- Key figures include William Wordsworth, Mary Shelley, Charlotte Brontë and John Keats.

Realism (mid-19th to early 20th century)

- Focused on depicting everyday life with accuracy.
- It often dealt with social issues and featured complex characters.
- Important players include Charles Dickens and Leo Tolstoy.

Modernism (late 19th to mid-20th century)

- Characterised by a departure from traditional forms, reflecting the fragmented state of society post-World War I.
- Virginia Woolf, James Joyce and T.S. Eliot are ones to watch – well, read.

Postmodernism (mid-20th century to present)
- Known for its sceptical view of narratives, blending reality and fiction, and questioning absolute truths.
- Margaret Atwood, Samuel Beckett and Kurt Vonnegut are good examples.

Analysing literary movements

1. **Identify key features:** Recognise the defining elements of each literary movement. Your text may contain only one or two. Position your text as a part of the movement by learning the key concerns.

2. **Historical and social context:** Explore the historical and social background of each movement. For example, Modernism occurred roughly at the end of World War I when the world was reeling from such a cataclysmic event – this is why modernist authors experimented with form. The rule book of the world had just been blown up, why not the rules around writing novels?!

3. **Comparative studies:** Compare works from the same or different movements to understand and learn their characteristics. Read a novel from the Romantic era, and some Wordsworth poems. What similarities do they share? Where do they differ? How do they convey the overwhelming emotion of the time?

Defining genre

While literary movements provide a historical and cultural context, genres are categories based on shared patterns, themes or styles. This section will explore various genres. I've chosen these genres as they seem the most common in the English and Literature classroom. Again, like literary movements, this list is not exhaustive. There's a plethora of genres and sub-genres out there.

Exploring different genres

- **Gothic:** Characterised by elements of horror, death, romance and mystery. The Gothic genre focuses on the inner workings of the human mind under pressure. The Gothic is often set in gloomy castles or landscapes. There's a mysterious atmosphere, supernatural elements and heightened emotions. Notable works in this genre include Mary Shelley's *Frankenstein* and Bram Stoker's *Dracula*.

- **Comedy:** Focuses on humour to entertain and often convey a message or critique of society. It includes sub-genres like satire, romantic comedy and slapstick. Classic examples are Shakespeare's *A Midsummer Night's Dream* and Oscar Wilde's *The Importance of Being Ernest*.

- **Action:** Centres on exciting and often physical activities. Action stories are fast-paced, involving adventures, conflicts and usually a hero facing challenges. Popular in cinema, action can also be found in literature, like Alexandre Dumas' *The Three Musketeers*.

- **Crime:** Revolves around the detection of a crime and its perpetrator. It often includes a detective or investigator unravelling the mystery. Classic examples are Arthur Conan Doyle's Sherlock Holmes series, and Agatha Christie's *Hercule Poirot* and *Miss Marple*.
- **Mystery:** Involves solving a puzzle or uncovering secrets, often overlapping with the crime genre. It builds suspense and engages readers in solving the mystery alongside the characters. Notable works include Edgar Allen Poe's detective stories and *The Girl with the Dragon Tattoo* by Stieg Larsson.
- **Magical realism:** Blends realistic narratives with fantastical elements. It's characterised by a grounded setting in which magical elements are viewed as normal. Famous examples include García Márquez's *One Hundred Years of Solitude* and Salman Rushdie's *Midnight's Children*.

Analysing genre

When beginning an analysis of your text through the lens of genre, these questions can offer a guide:

- What genre or genres does this text belong to? What specific conventions are used?
- How does using them shape the text's meaning and effect?
- How does the author endorse or challenge conventions?
- What are the roles and purposes of this specific genre?
- Does the text embrace or reject typical roles and purposes? How and why?
- What themes or arguments might the genre conventions bring attention to by nature of the category itself?
- How does using genre conventions enable discussing those themes?
- How do expectations around genre invite interpretation even before reading? How does the text meet, challenge or complicate those expectations?

Activity: Literary lens

Using the text you're studying, or one of the short stories from earlier, you will interpret it through two lenses: literary movement and genre.

Step 1: Identify the literary movement

- What period or school of thought does the text align with?
- Highlight words/passages in the text reflecting the movement's key ideas.

Step 2: Identify the genre/s

- What genre conventions does the story use?
- Circle descriptions, events, character types that align with a specific genre.

Step 3: Analyse through a movement lens

- Given the historical context, what ideas/questions might the author explore based on the movement?
- How does the knowledge of the movement shape your interpretation?

Step 4: Analyse through a genre lens

- How does the genre of your text shape the author's choices?
- In what ways does the text align with, or challenge, the genre?

Step 5: Connect interpretations

- Synthesise what you notice from both the movement and genre analysis. Do they align? Do they enrich each other? Have they offered new insights into your text?

CHAPTER 4

Unpacking form and meaning

In this chapter we will explore the relationship between form and a text's meaning. Part of your study of literature, and something you'll need to include in your literary analysis, is how the form of your text impacts the author's meaning. Remember: texts are constructions. The author of your text made deliberate choices about how their text was to be constructed and then presented to you, the reader. These choices impact what you take away from the text – it's meaning.

Understanding form

Form refers to the way the text is structured and organised. This can include the genre, the narrative structure, the use of verse or prose, and even the specific literary devices employed by the author. To understand form, consider the frame (or skeleton) of a building – it's the framework upon which everything else is built.

Examples of literary forms

Narrative structures

- Novels, novellas, short stories, fables.
- Linear and non-linear timeline approaches using flashbacks, flashforwards and unfolding perspectives differently.
- Plot trajectories build tension through exposition, rising action, climax and resolution stages.
- Frame narratives embed stories, use multiple narrators or shift narrative settings.
- Stream of conciousness abandons conventions to capture freewheeling throughts.

Poetic forms

- Sonnets, villanelles and sestinas rely on intricate repetition of lines and syllables.
- Odes, elegies, epic poems, dramatic monologues, ballads, free verse.
- Stanzas cluster verses into groups with shifts signalling thematic changes.
- Open-verse poetry has looser structural elements than closed forms.
- Shape and concrete poetry arrange words to literally illustrate ideas.

The play

- Tragedies, comedies, histories, absurdist plays.
- Acts and scenes time the storyline with character entrances and exits.
- Stage directions guide blocking while conveying inner processes.
- Monologues, soliloquies and asides reveal personal commentaries.
- Tragic versus comedic structures invoke different audience responses.

> **Non-fiction forms**

- Memoirs, biographies, autobiographies, diaries, letters, essays, speeches.
- Memoirs use narrative techniques like scenes, character development and plot arcs to structure stories based on real experiences.
- Essays present a focused thesis and logical evidence through standard expository paragraphs. Rhetorical techniques may be used persuasively.
- Historical accounts select and arrange factual and/or archival material to provide reconstructive reports.

Discovering meaning

Meaning in literature is the message or the underlying significance of the text. It's what the author wants to convey to the reader, be it an idea, a moral lesson or a reflection on society. Understanding the meaning involves peeling back the layers of a story to see what the author is trying to communicate beneath the surface.

Meaning can be explored through:

- **Themes:** These are the central ideas or messages in the work. No doubt you've heard your English or Literature teacher bang on about these non-stop. Some common and universal themes include love, loss or courage.
- **Character development:** The growth or changes in the characters can reveal a lot about the meaning of the text.
- **Author's background:** Sometimes, knowing about the author's life and times can help in understanding the deeper meaning of the text.
- **Setting:** The time and place your text are set can also impact its meaning.

The relationship between form and meaning

Understanding the relationship between form and meaning is essential in literary analysis. An author's choice of form can greatly influence the meaning of their work. For example, a poem written in a rigid, structured form might be used to convey themes of constraint and control. On the other hand, a free verse poem might be used to express freedom and fluidity.

Consider how form and meaning work together in these examples:

- **Shakespeare's sonnets:** The strict form of the sonnet, with its 14 lines and specific rhyme scheme, often contrasts with the deep emotional content of love, beauty and mortality.
- **Modernist novels:** Authors like Virginia Woolf and James Joyce broke traditional narrative structures to create stream-of-consciousness writing, mirroring the complexity of human thought. By breaking the traditional narrative structure, they were also reflecting the chaos of the modern world.

The way an author constructs their text impacts the meaning and the messages that we, as readers, take away from it. The more standard and regular forms tend to reinforce normal ideas and assumptions, while experimental forms mirror unexpected content that challenges literary traditions. For example, the classic five-paragraph essay structure with an introduction, three body paragraphs and a conclusion, lends an inherent logic, credibility and trust to the writer's belief. However, a persuasive piece written in an unusual formal, like a dialogue, poem or screenplay, makes the reader perceive that the same content differently by questioning preconceived beliefs that standard essay form supports.

In the creative non-fiction form, such as memoirs and personal essays, artistic language blurs facts and feelings, which can broaden the emotional impact. Descriptive details and expressive words stir up reactions. The styles and structures the author deliberately chooses influences how the reader ends up balancing truth and interpretation in their reading.

Remember, when studying literature, creative form and embedded meaning have an intricate relationship. An author's structural decisions influence far more than merely organising text on a page. These choices actively impact the message, transform perspective and breathe life into the text's themes through the reader's experience.

Activity: Unpacking form; unveiling meaning

Using the text you're studying, or one of the short stories listed earlier in this book, you're going to explore the relationship between form and meaning.

Step 1: Sticky notes

- Grab your text and sticky notes (teachers love sticky notes).

Step 2: Mark your evidence

- As you read, and re-read, use your sticky notes to mark specific elements of form that jump out at you. This could be anything you find interesting, such as:
  - Unusual word choices
  - Imagery
  - Striking sound devices (rhyme, rhythm, etc.)
  - Odd sentence structures
  - Dialogue and speech patterns
  - Narrative structures

Step 3: Question, question, question

- For each sticky note, write a question below it on the note itself. This question should explore how your chosen element might be contributing to the meaning of the text. Some example questions you might consider include:
  - How does this metaphor connect to the theme of loneliness?
  - Why does the author use such short sentences here?
  - What kind of mood does this rhyme scheme create?

Step 4: Connect the dots

- Take a step back and review your sticky notes and questions.
- Look for patterns or connections between different elements of form and their potential meaning.
- Reflect on how the overall use of form in the text shapes your understanding of it.

CHAPTER 5

Literature in context

Literature is shaped by its context; it is not created in a vacuum. Literature explores the historical, cultural and social environment in which it was written. Context can influence everything from the characters and their dialogue to the setting and the plot. It's like a lens that offers a unique view of the world through the author's eyes.

Understanding context enriches our reading experience. It allows us to see beyond the text and grasp the deeper meaning and themes. By considering the historical, cultural and social contexts, we can appreciate the complexity of literature and the universality of its themes, regardless of when or where it was written.

Historical context

Imagine reading a story set during World War II. The historical context here – World War II, its causes and its global impact – will significantly influence the story's setting, conflicts and themes. Similarly, a novel set in Melbourne in 2020 during the COVID-19 lockdowns will reflect the struggles of remote learning, QR codes, fear and worry, and the five-kilometre rule that people experienced during that time.

By understanding the historical period in which a book was written or set, we gain insights into the characters' motivations, the societal norms they followed and the challenges they faced. It helps us to understand why characters behave the way they do and why certain events unfold as they do.

Questions to consider – historical context

1. What historical events or periods are referenced in the text?
2. How do these events influence the characters and their actions?
3. What historical figures or movements are mentioned, and why are they significant?
4. How does the historical setting impact the text's conflicts and resolutions?
5. Are there any anachronisms (elements not true to the period) in the text, and what might their purpose be?

Tips for analysis – historical context

- Research the period your text is set it, and when the author wrote it.
- Look for historical references in the text, like dates, events, historical figures or technology.
- Consider how the historical context might influence the characters' worldviews and decisions.

Cultural context

Cultural context focuses on the customs, beliefs and societal norms that define a particular group or society. Literature often reflects the culture of its time. For instance, the works of Jane Austen intricately portray the manners and societal expectations of the British gentry during the early 19th century.

Cultural contexts can also include artistic movements, religious beliefs and dominant philosophies. For example, the existentialist movement influenced many writers in the 20th century to explore themes like freedom, individuality and the meaning of life.

Questions to consider – cultural context

1. What cultural norms and values are portrayed in the text?
2. How do these cultural aspects influence the characters' behaviours and beliefs?
3. Are there any cultural symbols, traditions or rituals mentioned? What is their significance?
4. How does the culture depicted compare to your own or other cultures?
5. Does the text challenge or reinforce cultural norms of its time?

Tips for analysis – cultural context

- Identify the culture or cultures represented in the text.
- Look for cultural references, such as language use, customs, clothing or food.
- Research the cultural background of the author and consider how this might influence the text.
- Explore how characters react to cultural norms – do they conform, rebel or struggle with them?

Social context

The social context of a text is closely tied to its historical and cultural context. It includes the social dynamics and structures at the time of writing or the time in which the story is set. This can encompass class structures, gender roles and racial dynamics.

For example, in *To Kill a Mockingbird* by Harper Lee, the social context of racial prejudice in the American South is crucial to understanding the story's conflict and themes. Similarly, Charles Dickens' novels often critique the social inequalities and injustices of Victorian England.

Questions to consider – social context

1. What social classes, roles or groups are represented in the text?
2. How do these social structures impact the characters and their interactions?
3. Are there any social issues or conflicts addressed in the text, such as inequality, discrimination or gender roles?
4. How do characters' social statuses influence their perspectives and opportunities?
5. Does the text seem to critique or support prevailing social structures of its time?

Tips for analysis – social context

- Identify the key social structures or hierarchies present in the text.
- Look for social conflicts and consider how they drive the plot or character development.
- Consider the social background of the author and how this might reflect in the text.
- Analyse how different characters respond to their social environment – are they conformists, rebels, victims or something else?

Context and the author's perspective

An author's background – their upbringing, experiences and the time they live in – greatly influences their writing. For example, Ernest Hemingway's experience as an ambulance driver in World War I is evident in his novels, which often explore themes of war, heroism and loss.

Similarly, Australian author Anna Funder's background imbues her writing. A child of a psychologist and a human rights lawyer, her works are concerned with human dignity, personal freedoms and oppression. Having spent time in East Berlin during and immediately after the fall of the Berlin Wall, her texts are concerned with life in communist East Germany. *Stasiland* concerns intimate stories, derived through Funder's interview technique, about life under the Stasi.

Activity: Exploring literature and context

This activity will help you to understand how knowing about the different contexts of the text you're studying can influence your interpretation and understanding of the text.

Step 1: Reading (what a shock!)

- Read your chosen text. Or, re-read it. You need to have a general understanding of the text, its characters, themes and ideas.

Step 2: Research

- Conduct some research into the contexts that are impacting your text:
  - **Historical context:** What historical events or conditions at the time of writing may influence the text?
  - **Cultural context:** What were the cultural norms, beliefs and artistic trends when the author wrote the text?
  - **Social context:** What were the societal structures and norms, class relations and social issues prevalent at the time?
  - **Authorial context:** What aspects of the author's own life experiences, beliefs and identity may have influenced their writing of the text?

Step 3: Reading and re-reading

- Re-read the text again, this time with a focus on identifying elements that reflect the contexts researched.

Step 4: Write it all down

♦ Write your observations down – this will help with your final literary analysis. Things you should cover in your notes and observations are:

- How each context (historical, cultural, social and authorial) is reflected in the text.
- An evaluation of how these contexts help in understanding the themes, characters and narrative of the text.
- Your personal thoughts and feelings on how the context changed or deepened your understanding of the text.

CHAPTER 6

Critical approaches to literature

When we read literature, we're not just engaging with the stories or characters. We're also encountering complex ideas, societal norms and varied human experiences. To explore these ideas in more nuanced ways, literary critics use various *lenses* known as critical theories. These theories help us to analyse texts in specific ways and look for specific things.

Feminist literary theory

Feminist criticism examines how texts reinforce or challenge the roles and representations of women. It seeks to uncover underlying biases and question traditional gender roles. This approach not only focuses on how female characters are portrayed, but also looks at the roles of female authors and readers.

Questions to consider

1. How are women represented in the text?
2. Does the narrative reinforce or challenge traditional gender roles?
3. How do the experiences of female characters differ from those of male characters?

Applying feminist theory

Consider Jane Austen's *Pride and Prejudice*. A feminist analysis might explore how the novel critiques the limited roles and expectations of women in 19th-century England, focusing on Elizabeth Bennet's resistance to societal norms.

Marxist literary theory

Marxist criticism views literature through the lens of socioeconomic class conflict. It examines how texts reflect, reinforce or challenge the inequalities of capitalist society. This approach is particularly interested in power dynamics and material conditions.

Questions to consider

1. How does the text depict class struggles?
2. Who holds the power or wealth, and how do they use it?
3. Does the text offer a critique of capitalism or social inequality?

Applying Marxist theory

Charles Dickens' *A Tale of Two Cities* can be examined through a Marxist lens, focusing on how it portrays the class struggle leading to the French Revolution and the plight of the oppressed under aristocratic rule.

Psychoanalytical theory

Psychoanalytical criticism draws on the theories of Sigmund Freud and others to explore the psychological dimensions of literature. This approach looks at the unconscious desires, fears and motivations of characters, as well as the psychological aspects of the author's own life.

Questions to consider

1. What are the unconscious motivations of the characters?
2. How do childhood experiences or primal desires influence the characters' actions?
3. Can any aspects of the author's own psychological profile be detected in the text?

Applying psychoanalytical theory

Shakespeare's *Hamlet* offers rich material for psychoanalytical analysis, particularly in exploring Hamlet's internal conflicts, his relationship with his mother and his indecisiveness, which may reflect deeper psychological issues.

Queer theory

Queer theory is a relatively modern field in literary criticism, emerging in the late 20th century. It questions and deconstructs traditional ideas about gender and sexuality, focusing on how literature portrays and challenges norms related to these concepts. This approach is particularly useful in exploring the representation of LGBTIQA+ characters, relationships and experiences in texts, as well as in analysing how sexuality and gender identity are constructed and understood.

Questions to consider

1. How does the text portray characters' gender identities and sexual orientations?
2. Does the narrative challenge or reinforce traditional gender and sexual norms?
3. How are LGBTIQA+ characters and themes treated in the text? Are they central or are they marginalised?

Applying queer theory

Virginia Woolf's *Orlando* is an excellent example for a queer theory analysis. The novel's exploration of gender fluidity, with the protagonist changing sex over centuries, challenges traditional notions of gender and sexuality, making it a ripe subject for a queer theoretical analysis.

Ecocriticism

Ecocriticism is a critical approach that explores the relationship between literature and the natural world. Emerging in the 1990s, it focuses on how literature portrays nature and addresses ecological issues, reflecting a growing awareness of environmental issues. This approach often highlights the interconnection between humans and the natural world and critiques the anthropocentric (human-centred) perspectives in literature.

Questions to consider

1. How is nature depicted in the text, and what is its significance?
2. Does the narrative address ecological issues or themes, such as sustainability, climate change or human impact on the environment?
3. How do characters interact with their natural surroundings, and what does this reveal about their relationship with the environment?

Applying ecocriticism

Margaret Atwood's *Oryx and Crake* offers a good example for applying ecocriticism. This work, set in a dystopian future, explores themes of genetic engineering, biotechnology and environmental collapse. Atwood's text offers an image of a world ravaged by human activity, where natural environments have been largely replaced by genetically engineered landscapes. It is the ideal text to practise your ecocritical analysis skills on.

Activity: Applying literary criticism

This activity will help you to sequentially use different critical approaches to your text. After each short analysis through the four lenses, you will understand how each perspective offers a different interpretation of the text.

Step 1: Read (AGAIN?!)

- Read your text, or an excerpt, of your text. Choose a section or chapter that you enjoyed, or that has some juicy content that you can analyse.

Step 2: Familiarise yourself with the theories

- Re-read this chapter to refresh your understanding of each theory and what to look for; you may need to conduct some independent research on each theory if you're a little hazy.

Step 3: Prep your workspace

- Grab an A3 or A4 piece of blank paper and fold it so you have four boxes. Label each box with the critical theory you'll be focusing on. I've used four theories here, which you can also use.

Step 4: Analysis

- Box 1: Feminist theory
  - Apply a feminist criticism to the text.
  - Look for themes on gender, power dynamics and the representation of women.
  - Jot down your thoughts in the box, using quotes to support your thinking.

- Box 2: Marxist theory
    - Apply a Marxist reading of the text.
    - Look for representations of class, capitalism and socioeconomic conflict.
    - Add your notes to box two, again, with supporting evidence.
- Box 3: Psychoanalytical theory
    - Apply a psychoanalytical lens.
    - Focus on the psychological elements of the text: character motivations, symbolic meanings.
    - Add your notes. Don't forget that evidence.
- Box 4: Queer theory
    - Apply a queer lens to the text.
    - Look for representations of diverse sexuality, gender identity and societal norms.
    - Add your findings, with your evidence.

Step 5: Comparative writing

- After completing all the boxes, write a summary comparing the insights you gained from each critical approach.
- Discuss how each perspective provided a unique lens through which to view your text, and how each lens offered you new insights into your text and your interpretation.

CHAPTER 7

Adapting and transforming literature

Literature is not static; it evolves and takes on new forms. This section explores how stories and ideas move from the original form into different artistic expressions. No doubt you're already aware of some of the biggest cinema hits that have been adapted and transformed from novels, graphic novels and comics. Think *The Lord of the Rings*, the Harry Potter series and the Marvel Cinematic Universe. All these blockbuster films originated in print.

Understanding adaptations

Adaptations involve reinterpreting and reshaping a literary work into a new medium. This process can bring new insights and perspectives to the original story, making it accessible to a broader audience. Adaptations also reflect the time and culture in which they are created, offering a contemporary lens to view timeless themes.

Adaptations serve several purposes:

♦ **Expand audience:** By translating a story into an accessible, engaging new format, more people can be exposed to the themes and ideas of the original work. Shakespeare's *Romeo and Juliet* has been adapted several times, which allows for younger audiences to enjoy its timeless themes of love and loss.

♦ **Modern interpretation:** Adaptations reframe classic stories through contemporary lenses, making the themes, characters and emotions resonate powerfully with current audiences. Again, with Shakespeare, his play *The Taming of the Shrew* was adapted and transformed into the hit 1990s film *Ten Things I Hate About You*. A classic among the teen romcom, coming-of-age genre.

♦ **Showcase medium:** Each medium has its strength – from imaginative world building in novels to the dynamic visuals we see in films. Adaptations highlight iconic stories in innovative formats.

Key aspects of adaptations

1. **Fidelity to source material:** How closely does the adaptation follow the original work? Does it maintain the core themes and message, or does it diverge significantly? When engaging with an adaptation like this, you're engaging in *fidelity criticism*.

2. **Creative interpretation:** How does the adaptation add to or change the original story? This could involve modernising the setting, altering the characters to reflect modern sensibilities or introducing new themes.

3. **Cultural and temporal context:** How does the adaptation reflect the culture and time in which it was created?

Types of adaptations

1. **Film adaptations:** Books often find a new life on screen. For example, Harper Lee's *To Kill a Mockingbird* was adapted into a film that captured the essence of the novel while making it accessible to a wider audience.

2. **Stage adaptations:** Many works of literature, like Shakespeare's plays, are adapted for the theatre, offering a new dimension through live performance. In fact, some theorists posit that any printed script that is performed on stage is an adaptation.

3. **Graphic novel adaptations:** Adaptations aren't always about the silver screen, sometimes classic works of literature like Charles Dickens' *A Christmas Carol*, Mary Shelley's *Frankenstein* and Herman Melville's *Moby Dick* have been transformed into graphic novels, providing a visual narrative that appeals to different audiences.

4. **Musical/opera adaptations:** Spanning from tragedies like *The Phantom of the Opera* to comedies like *The Producers*, musicals bring sound and drama to all genres of literature. In 2024, the film *Mean Girls* has been adapted to a *Mean Girls* musical. Adding songs and musical cues further develop the text's themes and ideas.

5. **Video games adaptation:** The latest trend in adapting and transforming literature has been in video games. Recent interactive games like *The Witcher* and *Cyberpunk 2077* immerse players in extensive story worlds based on science fiction and fantasy novels.

Challenges of adapting literature

Adaptations aim to capture the most pivotal and powerful moments of a story within the conventions of another medium. This involves navigating key challenges. These are the kinds of things you need to consider if writing an analysis of how your text has been adapted:

Tone
- Matching the emotional resonance and nuanced tone of complex literary works poses difficulties, especially in shorter formats.

Condensing stories
- Long, intricate novels have to be carefully condensed, interweaving plotlines and extensive world development into a two-hour film, while retaining the essence of the original text.

Character motivation
- Showcasing the multidimensional perspectives and motivations of all characters in a new medium often requires narrative sacrifices. Consider: as a reader we have access to a character's thoughts – how does that translate onto the screen?

Fan expectations
- Passionate book fans have preconceived visions that influence their reception of reimagined characters and plot points. Their expectations are difficult to fully satisfy.

Activity: Adapting literature

This short activity will give you some insight into the decisions that authors, poets, film directors, producers and screenwriters go through when they wrangle with adapting a text.

Step 1: Select and analyse a text

- Using the text you're studying, or another text, select a specific element to focus on (a character, theme, scene, etc.).
- Closely analyse this element for its key ideas, descriptions, themes.

Step 2: Choose a new medium or form

- Select a different medium or form to adapt your element into. This could be a short story into a script for a play, a poem into a visual art, a novel excerpt into a short film concept.

Step 3: Create the adaptation

- Using the chosen medium, creatively adapt your element of the literary work. This might involve writing a script, drawing a series of comic panels, outlining a film storyboard or composing a series of poems.

Step 4: Reflect on the process

- Write a brief reflection on the adaptation process. Consider:
  - How did you interpret the original work in your adaptation?
  - What were the challenges and creative decisions involved in transforming the work into a new medium?
  - How does the new form change the way the original work is experienced or understood?

CHAPTER 8

Writing a literary analysis

A literary, or close, analysis is a crucial skill for any student studying literature. This chapter will guide you through the process of crafting a thoughtful, well-structured literary analysis essay. A literary analysis essay involves closely examining a text to discuss how various components contribute to its overall meaning or effect.

The purpose of a literary analysis

The goal of a literary analysis is to break down a piece of literature and understand its elements, such as themes, characters, plot and stylistic devices. It's about exploring why the author made certain choices and how these choices contribute to the overall message or impact of the work.

Reader before writer – the pre-writing phase

Before you can confidently write about your text, you need to read it. This may seem like I'm pointing out the obvious, but the study of literature is, at its core, about reading. No doubt you've read your text once, a reading for pleasure. You either liked or disliked your text. Perhaps you found it exciting, perhaps a bore. Well, first, congratulations. You've completed a very simple, succinct response to the text.

Writing a literary analysis requires a bit more than that, in fact, a lot more. You need to read, and then re-read your text. You need to actively engage with it. Here are some strategies that you may want to use to actively engage with your text:

1. **Annotate the text:** If you own the book, don't be scared to mark it up, highlighting or underlining key moments, words or your personal reactions to the text. As you re-read, you'll come across your own annotations and may add to them, perhaps answering your own question. All these scribblings will help you with your literary analysis.

2. **Brainstorming ideas:** Grab a blank piece of paper or your exercise book. Begin to scribble. Freely jotting down ideas encourages you to 'brain dump' whatever comes to mind as you read. You don't need to worry about spelling or grammar. Just get whatever comes into your mind onto the page.

3. **Listing:** You may find it helpful to write lists, all the lists. Focus on a character and list their traits, your response to them, any supporting evidence. Perhaps a moment in the text: what happened? How did it happen? What led to this happening?

4. **Ask questions:** As you read, ask questions – and write them down. Ask yourself questions about the plot, the characters, the title. Are they believable? What does it all add up to? What does the story mean to you?

5. **Keep a journal:** As you read your text, jot down your thoughts. This could be done at the end of the last class, documenting the discussion. Or it could be done after reading a whole chapter. What happened? Who was involved? Your reaction to the text?

Reader becomes writer – writing your analysis

Structuring the analysis

- **Introduction**
  - Start with an engaging opening that introduces the text and the author.
  - Present your main contention, outlining the main argument of your essay.

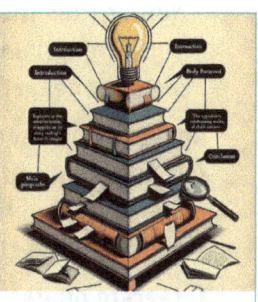

- **Body paragraphs**
  - Each paragraph should focus on one idea or point.
  - Provide evidence from the text and then explain how it supports your points.

- **Conclusion**
  - Summarise your main points and restate your main contention.
  - Discuss the broader implications of your analysis and why it's important.

Writing the analysis

- **Close reading**
  - Pay close attention to the text.
  - Look for patterns, contrasts and literary techniques.
  - Explain how these elements contribute to the overall theme or message.

- **Critical thinking**
  - Interpret, analyse and critique the literary elements.
  - Ask yourself why the author used certain words/techniques and consider the impact on the reader.

Supporting your arguments

- **Use evidence**
  - Support your arguments with direct quotes from the text.
  - This strengthens your analysis and shows a close engagement with the text.

- **Analyse, don't summarise**
  - Focus on interpretation rather than just summarising the plot or the content of the text.
  - Your analysis should offer new insights.

- **Integrate quotes smoothly**
  - The quote from the text should form a part of your sentence. It shouldn't just sit there doing nothing as a standalone sentence. Make it part of your work.

Refining your essay

- **Review and revise**
  - Re-read your essay to check for clarity and coherence.
  - Make sure each paragraph is one idea and that your argument flows logically.

- **Edit for grammar and punctuation**
  - Pay attention to grammar, punctuation and writing style.
  - A well-written analysis should be easy to read, authoritative (no slang or contractions) and persuasive. Sell your case!

- **Seek feedback**
  - Get feedback from peers, teachers or tutors.
  - Fresh perspectives can help you identify areas for improvement.

Writing a literary analysis is about more than just reviewing the text; it's a chance to engage in a deeper conversation with the literature. By carefully examining and interpreting the text, and presenting your analysis in a structured, well-argued essay, you contribute to a broader understanding of the work.

CHAPTER 9

Responding creatively to literature

A creative response to literature allows you to go beyond traditional literary analysis and engage with texts in a more personal and imaginative way. This chapter explores how you can craft your own creative responses to literature, expressing your understanding and interpretation of key themes, ideas, views and values present in the original work.

The value of creative responses

Creative responses to literature enable you to explore and express your interpretation in unique ways. This allows for a deeper connection with the text and allows for the exploration of its themes and ideas through different mediums, such as writing, visual arts or performance.

Methods of creative response

The great thing about the creative response is that the options are limitless; you can essentially do what you want. The issue is that too much choice causes confusion. What do I do?! Here are some ideas, but don't limit yourself to these:

- **Creative writing:** You can write a poem, short story or monologue inspired by a theme or character from the text. This will allow you to explore the narrative from a new perspective or to delve deeper into a particular aspect of the text.

- **Visual arts:** Creating artwork – be it a painting, sculpture or digital art – in response to your text can capture the mood, themes or imagery of the text. This approach appeals to visually oriented students and provides a platform for non-verbal expressions.

- **Performance:** Dramatising a scene or embodying a character through performance enables students to engage with the text physically and emotionally. This can be done through acting, dance or even musical composition.

- **Filling in a gap:** Write a story, poem or dialogue that fills in a narrative gap and further explores the ideas and themes of the text. This could be telling the story of a minor character or describing an event that is only alluded to in the original text.

- **Giving a voice to the voiceless:** Create a piece that brings a silent perspective to the forefront. This might involve writing from the point of view of a marginalised character or exploring a theme that the text touches on but doesn't fully address.

Crafting a creative response

When crafting your creative response, consider the following:

Choose an element	Interpret and imagine	Select a medium	Create and reflect
• Select a specific theme, character or scene from the text that resonates with you.	• Think about how this element speaks to you. • What does it say about human nature, society or the world? • Use your imagination and explore these ideas.	• Decide how you want to express your response – through writing, art or performance.	• Create your piece, keeping in mind the original text and your interpretation of it. • Reflect on how this process has deepened your understanding of the text.

Responding creatively to literature 71

CHAPTER 10

Preparing for your exam

Your end-of-year English and/or Literature exams are a significant part of your final year. If you're in Victoria, you must complete one of these exams. A subject from the English group is compulsory, after all. (How annoying for you – but great for me because it keeps me in a job!) In this chapter, we'll go over some things to get you ready for your exam.

The exam format and assessment criteria

Before getting into your revision, it is important to familiarise yourself with what you're being asked to do. This will help you tailor your studies and understand what the examiners are looking for. Here are some ways to approach this:

- **Review the study design:** In Victoria, the Victoria Curriculum and Assessment Authority study designs for English and Literature provide a detailed breakdown of the exam structure, assessment criteria and the knowledge and skills required for each exam. If you're based in a different state, ask your teacher if there is a similar approach where you live. You can also ask your teacher for their insights into the exam. Another approach is to join Facebook groups and Reddits to hear from current and past students.

- **Examiner's reports:** Access the previous year's examiner's report. These offer valuable insights into what assessors pick up on, what not to do and what to do. There are also sample responses you can read to see what a high-level response looks like.

- **Practice exams:** There are heaps of companies out there that create practice exams. If your school isn't buying them, then you can buy straight from the supplier. You can also access previous years' exams to see and practise with a range of topics.

Planning your revision

Effective time management is essential for exam success. Create a structured revision schedule to ensure you adequately cover all the required content and skills. Here are some things to think about for your schedule:

- **Break it down:** Divide the weeks leading up to the exams into smaller, manageable chunks. Create a revision schedule that allocates specific time slots for studying different aspects of the exam.

- **Re-read your texts:** Once you've settled on which texts you're going to write on, re-read them! A solid knowledge of the text will help you to respond to any topic that you may get in the exam – even the curly ones.

- **Be realistic:** Don't be too overambitious. You won't stick to huge plans. You also won't stick to your revision plans if you don't give yourself time to relax, see friends, attend parties.

Text revision strategies

Actively revise your text to deepen your understanding and knowledge of the text. Some ways to do this include:

- **Text analysis practice:** Analyse passages from your texts, focusing on language techniques, character development, themes and the connection between form and meaning. Practise writing detailed annotations, highlighting important elements and connections within the text.

- **Essay writing:** Hone your essay-writing skills by practising different essay topics and question types. Focus on developing clear arguments, using evidence effectively and writing in a clear style.

- **Handwriting practice:** One of the biggest issues with exams is understanding handwriting. If your assessor can't read what you've written, then they can't give you all the marks! Practise all your essays under timed conditions, and make sure they're handwritten. It's a skill, and all skills need practice.

- **Create resources:** Summarise key plot points, character traits, themes and important quotes from your texts. Make flashcards with literary terms and definitions. These resources will be invaluable for quick revision closer to the exam.

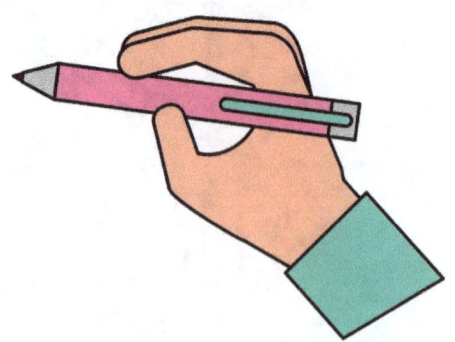

Conclusion

Congratulations! You've made it to the end of this book. By now, you should have a solid toolkit of strategies to tackle any text that comes your way. Remember, literary analysis is all about diving deep into the story, exploring the nooks and crannies of language, character, theme and context. It's your chance to have a conversation with the text and express your unique perspective.

As you gear up for exams and assessments, stay chill, stay focused and, most importantly, keep reading! The more books you devour, the sharper your analytical skills will become. Plus, you'll discover even more amazing stories, characters and friends along the way.

www.ingramcontent.com/pod-product-compliance
Lightning Source LLC
Chambersburg PA
CBHW070330120526
44590CB00017B/2846